COOL
FORENSIC TOOLS
Technology at Work

ESTHER BECK

ABDO
Publishing Company

VISIT US AT WWW.ABDOPUBLISHING.COM

Published by ABDO Publishing Company, 8000 West 78th Street, Edina, Minnesota 55439.
Copyright © 2009 by Abdo Consulting Group, Inc. International copyrights reserved in all countries.
No part of this book may be reproduced in any form without written permission from the publisher.
The Checkerboard Library™ is a trademark and logo of ABDO Publishing Company.

Printed in the United States.
Design and Production: Mighty Media, Inc.
Art Direction: Kelly Doudna
Photo Credits: Kelly Doudna, Ablestock, iStockPhoto (Bertrand Collet, Viktor Gmyria, Rob Howarth), ShutterStock
Series Editor: Pam Price
The following manufacturers/names appearing in this book are trademarks: Quaker

Library of Congress Cataloging-in-Publication Data

Beck, Esther.
   Cool forensic tools : technology at work / Esther Beck.
      p. cm. -- (Cool CSI)
   Includes index.
   ISBN 978-1-60453-486-3
   1. Forensic sciences--Juvenile literature. 2. Criminal
investigation--Juvenile literature. I. Title.

   HV8073.8.B43 2009
   363.25--dc22

                            2008023818

TO ADULT HELPERS

You're invited to assist up-and-coming forensic investigators! And it will pay off in many ways. Your children can develop new skills, gain confidence, and do some interesting projects while learning about science. What's more, it's going to be a lot of fun!

These projects are designed to let children work independently as much as possible. Let them do whatever they are able to do on their own. Also encourage them to keep a CSI journal. Soon, they will be thinking like real investigators.

So get out your magnifying glass and stand by. Let your young investigators take the lead. Watch and learn. Praise their efforts. Enjoy the scientific adventure!

CONTENTS

fingerprint

shoe print

fibers

FUN WITH FORENSICS

So you want to know more about crime scene investigation, or CSI. Perhaps you saw a crime solvers show on television and liked it. Or maybe you read about an ace investigator in a favorite **whodunit** book. Now you're curious, how do the investigators solve crimes?

The answer is *forensic science*. This term means science as it relates to the law. The many areas of forensic science can help link people to crimes, even if there are no eyewitnesses. Forensic scientists look at the evidence left at a crime scene and try to figure out what happened there.

tool marks

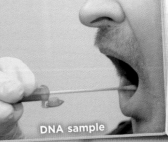
DNA sample

chemical residue

Evidence can include fingerprints, shoe prints, and fibers. It can include DNA samples from blood and saliva, tool marks, and chemical residue. Often this evidence can be quite small. In the CSI business, this is known as trace evidence. But even the smallest evidence can place a suspect at a crime scene.

Crime scene investigators **analyze** the evidence. Then they try to answer these questions about a crime.

1. What happened?
2. Where and when did it occur?
3. Who are the suspects, and why did they do it?
4. How was the crime done?

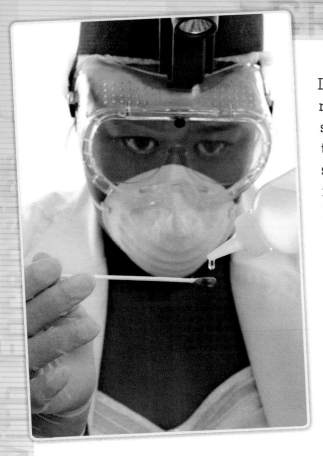

Different kinds of evidence require different kinds of scientists to find the answers to these questions. Forensic scientists specialize in fields such as chemistry, biology, physics, engineering, psychology, and even **entomology** and **botany**.

All these scientists use common sense and old-fashioned observation. They also rely on high-tech equipment and the latest scientific discoveries. Most important, forensic scientists use the scientific method.

Investigators begin by observing the crime scene. They then predict what happened and, if possible, who committed the crime based on the evidence.

Next they test the evidence. Their test results may support their predictions. Or, the results may tell them that their predictions were not correct.

Finally, they draw a conclusion about what happened. They may decide that further testing is required.

In this book series, you'll have a chance to test your own crime-solving talent. You'll do some challenging hands-on forensics activities. Each book in the series covers a specific area of CSI. In addition to this book, *Cool Forensic Tools: Technology at Work*, be sure to check out:

- *Cool Biological Clues: What Hair, Bones, and Bugs Tell Us*
- *Cool Crime Scene Basics: Securing the Scene*
- *Cool Eyewitness Encounters: How's Your Memory?*
- *Cool Physical Evidence: What's Left Behind*
- *Cool Written Records: The Proof Is in the Paper*

Altogether, these books show how crime scene investigators use science to **analyze** evidence and solve crimes.

Whoduzit in Whodunits: Forensic Psychologists

Psychologists study minds and behavior. Forensic psychologists study the minds and behavior of crime suspects. They try to determine motive, or why a person may have committed a crime. They may try to determine whether a person was sane when he or she committed a crime.

F211A
CSI LAB

The Scientific Method

Forensic scientists aren't the only ones who use the scientific method. All scientists do.

The scientific method is a series of steps that scientists follow when trying to answer a question about how the world works. Here are the basic steps of the scientific method.

1. Observe. Pay attention to how something works.

2. Predict. Make a simple statement that explains what you observed.

3. Test. Design an experiment that tests your prediction. You need a good idea of what data to gather during the test. A good test has more than one trial and has controlled variables.

4. Conclude. Compare the data and make a conclusion. This conclusion should relate to your prediction. It will either support the prediction or tell you that your prediction was incorrect.

COOL CSI JOURNAL

Taking notes is important when you collect evidence as a crime scene investigator. Writing down facts helps crime scene investigators remember all the details of a crime scene later, when a crime is tried in court.

At the beginning of each activity in this book, there is a section called "Take Note!" It contains suggestions about what to record in your CSI journal. You can predict what you think will happen when you test evidence. And you can write down what did happen. Then you can draw a conclusion.

As you do experiments, record things in your journal. You will be working just like a real forensic scientist.

TAKE NOTE!

Get out your CSI journal when you see this box. "Take Note!" may have questions for you to answer about the project. There may be a suggestion about how to look at the project in a different way. There may even be ideas about how to organize the evidence you find. Your CSI journal is the place to keep track of everything!

SAFE SCIENCE

Good scientists practice safe science. Here are some important things to remember.

- Check with an adult before you begin any project. Sometimes you'll need an adult to buy materials or help you handle them for a while. For some projects, an adult will need to help you the whole time. The instructions will say when an adult should assist you.
- Ask for help if you're unsure about how to do something.
- If something goes wrong, tell an adult immediately.
- Read the list of things you'll need. Gather everything before you begin working on a project.
- Don't taste, eat, or drink any of the materials or the results unless the directions say that you can.
- Use protective gear. Scientists wear safety goggles to protect their eyes. They wear gloves to protect their hands from chemicals and possible burns. They wear aprons or lab coats to protect their clothing.
- Clean up when you are finished. That includes putting away materials and washing containers, work surfaces, and your hands.

COOL FORENSIC TOOLS: TECHNOLOGY AT WORK

This book is all about technology. The word *technology* means scientific knowledge used in a certain field or industry. In the computer field, technology is anything that makes computers run better and faster. It also refers to new programs designed for work or entertainment. In this book, the word *technology* refers to the field of crime solving, or forensic science.

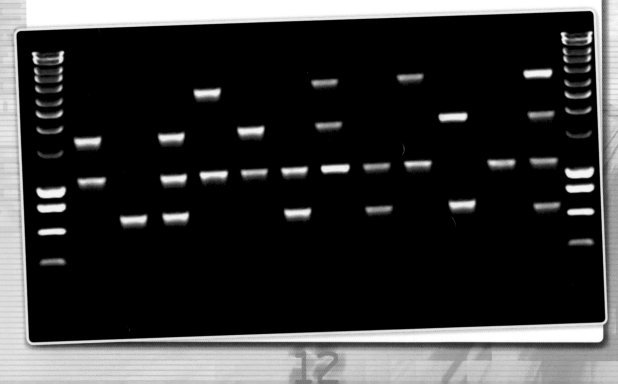

Today DNA **profiling** is probably the most talked about forensic technology. In just a few decades, it changed the crime-solving business. What exactly is so important about DNA matching?

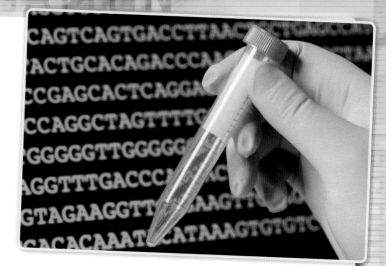

For starters, DNA is a kind of molecule that exists in each cell of living things. This molecule tells the cell how to grow. With the exception of identical twins, certain parts of everyone's DNA are **unique**. So, like fingerprints, DNA can be **analyzed** and linked to a specific person.

Both the criminal and the victim at a crime scene could leave behind DNA evidence. Investigators hope to match the DNA of a suspect to samples found at the crime scene. DNA technology is incredibly precise. So when a match occurs, juries know that they can trust the evidence.

Investigators use other kinds of technology too. They began using photography as early as 1864. Today, investigators still use photos to identify criminals and record crime scenes. Some photos of crime scenes may be used at trial. Juries can better understand crime scenes by viewing photos.

Forensic scientists rely on optics to do their work. Optics is the study of light and matter. At the crime scene, for example, they use **ultraviolet** (UV) light. This tool reveals hidden evidence that can't be seen under normal conditions.

Back at the lab, they use different microscopes to view trace evidence. Standard compound microscopes, like those used in schools, are common. Forensic scientists also use comparison microscopes. These let them look at two pieces of trace evidence at once. Scanning electron microscopes offer close-up views of elements that are too small for the eye to see.

When you talk tech, you can't forget computers. Computers help investigators organize data. The Internet connects crime solvers around the world. Sharing information about criminals can help investigators solve crimes quickly.

All of this equipment helps forensic scientists do their jobs efficiently. With the activities in this book, you'll have the opportunity to try out some of this technology. As you work, try to think of other high-tech tools. How might they be used to help crime solvers? The future of forensic science depends on good ideas, just like yours!

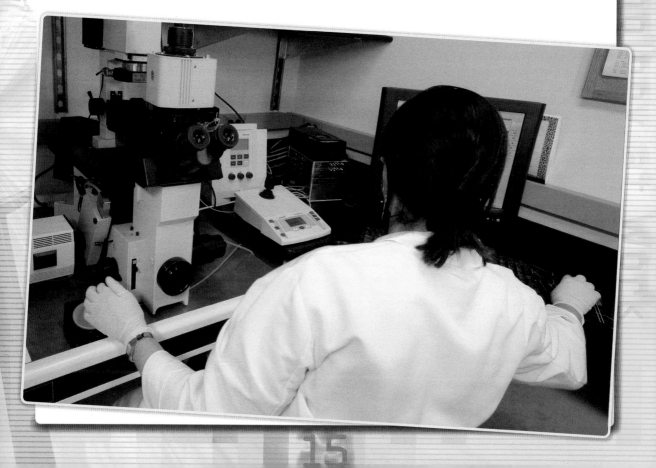

DNA EXTRACTION

THE CRIME SCENE: Your cousin agrees to babysit while your parents are out of town for the weekend. She's studying in college to become a crime scene investigator! At bedtime, she insists that you all pick up every last thing, including those dirty socks on the floor. Nobody claims the socks. Your cousin threatens to run DNA tests on the dead skin cells in the socks. She says this test will determine whom they belong to. Could that be true?

DNA is a kind of molecule that exists in each cell of living things. This molecule tells the cell how to grow. In this activity, you will **extract** DNA from a strawberry and a kiwifruit.

MATERIALS

- rubbing alcohol
- three clean jars
- water
- shampoo (without conditioner)
- salt
- strawberry
- sturdy plastic zipper bags
- cheesecloth
- funnel
- wood barbecue skewers or wood coffee stirrers
- kiwifruit

TAKE NOTE!

Use your CSI journal to keep notes about your DNA extraction. Did the strawberry and kiwifruit DNA look similar? Describe your results.

1. Place the rubbing alcohol in the freezer for one hour to cool it.

2. In a jar, mix 1 cup (236.6 ml) of water with 1½ tablespoons (22.2 ml) of shampoo and ¾ teaspoon (4.6 g) of salt. This mixture is called the extraction buffer.

3. Place a strawberry in a plastic bag and close the bag. Mash the berry with your fingers for about two minutes.

4. Put 1 tablespoon (14.8 ml) of the extraction buffer into the bag and mix it with the berry for one minute.

5. Put a double layer of cheesecloth in the funnel. Place the funnel in a clean jar.

CSI TIP

DNA **profiling** can clear innocent people who've been accused of crimes. Sometimes these people are already in jail, serving time for crimes they did not commit. When the old evidence is retested with new technology, they are found innocent. Technology really pulls through for them!

THINK CSI

Forensic scientists first used DNA profiling to solve a crime in 1986. They compare DNA found at a crime scene with exemplar DNA. Exemplars are samples that investigators hope to match. An exemplar might be from a suspect, for example. DNA profiling works because, except for identical twins, parts of every person's DNA are **unique**.

6. Pour the strawberry mixture into the funnel. Let it drain through the cheesecloth.

7. Remove the funnel. The strained strawberry mixture should look like a pink liquid.

8. Gently pour 2 tablespoons (29.6 ml) of rubbing alcohol onto the strawberry mixture. Do not stir the liquids!

9. Two layers will form. The DNA is the stringy, cloudy-looking matter that rises to the top.

10. Use a wooden skewer or stirrer to try to pick up the DNA.

11. Repeat the steps above with kiwifruit. Or have a friend do one extraction while you do the other.

12. Compare the two DNA samples, looking at them closely.

EVEN MORE TO EXPLORE

You need special equipment to compare DNA molecules. But you can compare barcodes, which resemble DNA **profiles**. Collect barcodes from empty boxes and have someone photocopy one for you. Can you match the bars and spaces on the copy to one of your barcodes?

DATA HEADS

THE CRIME SCENE: Your school is buzzing! A thief has been stealing kids' coats, hats, and gym clothes from lockers. Eventually the trickster places the items in the lost and found closet. Now the closet is overflowing. When students come to claim items, it's a real mess.

Your math teacher offers to help organize things. She says your class can use what it knows about data organization. That gets you wondering, Can organizing evidence help solve a crime? In this activity, you will organize data to make it easier to find.

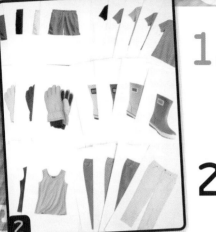

1. Find 25 pictures of different pieces of clothing in the catalogs or sales flyers. You should be able to easily describe each item, such as blue pants, red hat, and so on.

2. Tape or glue each picture to an index card. If you can't find pictures, you can draw the clothing items with colored pencils. Sketch one item per card.

TAKE NOTE!

Use your CSI journal or a computer with spreadsheet software to make a data table like this one. Keep notes on how it helps you locate information. How does that compare to finding information in unorganized data? Which method do you recommend?

Data Heads chart.xls

Item Number	Color									Item description							Boy's or Girl's Item?	
	red	blue	yellow	green	purple	orange	black	white	pink	pants	shirt	skirt	boots	socks	hat	gloves	boy	girl
1.			X										X				X	
2.	X									X							X	
3.		X																X
4.					X							X						X
5.	X														X		X	
Etc.															X		X	

Sheet1 Sheet2 Sheet3

Data Heads

2

3. Make a data table similar to the one shown in "Take Note!" Draw your table in a notebook or use a spreadsheet program on a computer. Yours will contain information about the 25 clothing items on your index cards.

4. First you'll time how long it takes to find information in unorganized data. Scatter the cards facedown on the floor.

5. Give your friend a list of the items. Start the stopwatch as your friend calls out an item, such as yellow rain boots. Flip over cards until you find the boots. Put each card facedown again before turning over another one.

6. When you find an item, have your friend call out another item. Stop the stopwatch after the fifth item. Record your time.

7. Next you'll search organized data. Start the stopwatch and have your friend call out five new items. Look for the items in your data table and write down their item numbers. For example, in the table in "Take Note!" the purple hat is item 4. After finding the fifth item, record your time.

8. Compare your times. Which method worked best? Does organizing data up front save time in the end?

MAGNIFICENT MAGNIFICATION

THE CRIME SCENE: You receive an interesting note in the mail. It might be a birthday party invitation, but it's hard to tell. The writing is so little that you can't read it!

You consider how you might best see the letters. You could borrow grandma's reading glasses. But she lives across town. Another idea is to use a magnifying glass. Will this tool make the super small appear extra tall?

In this activity, you will use magnifying lenses to view super small things.

MATERIALS

Equipment
- magnifying lenses of different strengths (2×, 6×, 10×, and 12×, for example)
- white paper
- black paper
- flashlight

Items to view
- several paper samples
- natural fiber samples such as wool, cotton, and linen
- man-made fiber samples such as polyester, rayon, and nylon
- hair samples from different people and pets
- fingernail clippings
- your own fingers and toes

TAKE NOTE!
Use your CSI journal to make notes about your observations. How did the appearance of the items change as you changed lenses?

1. Use a magnifying lens to view an item from the materials list. If the item is dark colored, place it on white paper. If the item is light colored, place it on black paper.

2. Repeat step 1 several times using lenses of different strengths.

3. Experiment with a light source. Use the flashlight to **illuminate** the item from different angles.

4. Repeat steps 1 through 3, choosing a different item to view.

5. Continue the above process until you've studied all the items from the list.

EVEN MORE TO EXPLORE

If you have access to a microscope, you can expand this activity. View the same materials under a 50×, 100×, or 200× microscope. What are you able to see that you couldn't see with a magnifying lens? Describe and sketch your observations in your CSI journal.

THINK CSI

Crime scene investigators use microscopes to examine trace evidence such as hair, fibers, glass, and paint. These are some of the microscopes they use.

compound microscope - magnifies up to 1,000 times.

comparison microscope - lines up two compound microscopes to view two pieces of evidence at once.

stereoscopic microscope - provides a 3-D view.

scanning electron microscope - beams of electrons provide high magnification.

MAKE A PINHOLE CAMERA

THE CRIME SCENE: Your teacher is upset! Yesterday she spent two hours arranging a bulletin board in your classroom. This morning, the design is on the floor! She suspects the nighttime janitor made the mess by accident. Or possibly the wind blew in through an open window.

Luckily, she had taken a quick snapshot of the finished bulletin board because she liked it so much. Now she shoots another to document the crime scene. Perhaps the photos will help determine who is to blame, the cleaning crew or the breeze.

In this activity, you'll build a simple pinhole camera and use it to shoot a room in your house, as if it were a crime scene.

MATERIALS

- newspaper
- round oatmeal box
- utility knife
- black paint (dull, not shiny)
- paintbrush
- scissors
- aluminum foil
- pin
- tape
- roll of 120 size 400 speed black-and-white film
- stopwatch or watch with a second hand
- adult helper

TAKE NOTE!

Investigators keep thorough notes while taking photographs at crime scenes. You can too. Write notes about the photos you take in your CSI journal. Later, match the pictures to the descriptions.

1. Spread the newspaper on your work surface.

2. Remove all the oatmeal from the box. Clean out any dust remaining in the box. Ask an adult to cut a 1-inch (2.5-cm) square in the side of the box.

3. Paint the inside and outside of the box black. Let it dry.

4. Cut a 2-inch (5-cm) square piece of aluminum foil. Use the pin to poke a tiny hole in the center of the square. This is where the pinhole camera gets its name!

5. Tape the foil square over the hole in the side of the box. Make sure the foil is secure. The only place light should enter the box is through the pinhole.

Whoduzit in Whodunits: Forensic Photographer

Forensic photographers take pictures of evidence before it is removed. They must record the crime scene without changing anything. Forensic photographers work with a variety of cameras, lenses, flash equipment, and filters. Forensic photographers are definitely tech savvy! Sometimes they even help determine whether other people's photos are real.

6. Take your camera, tape, scissors, adult helper, and the roll of film into a dark closet and shut the door. Be careful not to expose the film to light during the following steps.

7. Unroll some film from the roll. Have your helper use scissors to cut off a 4-inch strip of film.

8. Tape this film inside the oatmeal box, opposite the pinhole. Put the lid back on the box and tape it shut.

9. As you leave the closet, place a finger over the pinhole to block light from entering the camera.

Note: this photo shows where to put the film while you are working in the closet. Do not expose your film to light as we have done!

Think CSI

Photography is an important way of documenting crime scenes. Crime scene photographs help investigators piece together what happened at a scene. And they often serve as exhibits in court.

Forensic photographers arrive at crime scenes early and stay until the scene is processed. First they shoot establishing photographs to capture the entire scene. The outside of a house and entire rooms are examples. Then they snap midrange photos to capture details and show where the evidence was. Finally, they take close-up photographs to record the evidence in detail.

10. Keeping your finger over the pinhole, move the camera to where you'd like to take a picture. Set the camera on a table to steady it. Point the pinhole toward the subject.

11. Remove your finger from the pinhole. Expose the film for 60 seconds.

12. Place your finger on the pinhole again and return to the closet. Don't forget to close the door!

13. Remove the piece of film from the camera and place it inside the plastic film case that the film came in.

14. Take the film to be developed and printed.

15. Pick up the film and see how you did.

16. Try again with another piece of unexposed film.

EVEN MORE TO EXPLORE

If you have access to a digital camera, here's something fun to try. Shoot a scene from several angles. Download the images onto your computer and compare them side by side. Can you see how changing the perspective changes what you can see?

LIGHTS OUT!

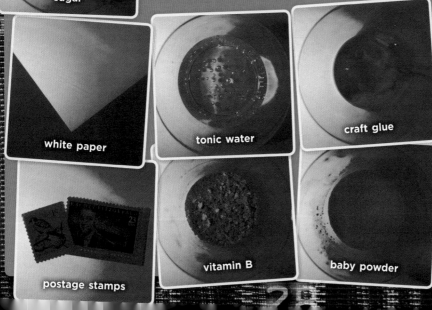

laundry detergent

sugar

white paper

tonic water

craft glue

vitamin B

baby powder

postage stamps

THE CRIME SCENE: On a field trip to a local theater, your class makes a startling discovery. When the lights dim and the curtain rises, a purplish light from the stage makes some students glow in the dark! But not everybody shines. What's up? Does anyone really know what makes someone glow?

In this activity, you'll use a black light to determine which materials are fluorescent. This experiment mirrors how crime scene investigators use special kinds of lights to solve crimes.

MATERIALS

Equipment
- black light lightbulb (can be purchased at a hardware store)
- portable lamp
- paper or plastic cups
- pen

Items to view
- powdered laundry detergent
- sugar
- white paper
- tonic water
- craft glue
- postage stamps
- crushed vitamin B
- baby powder

TAKE NOTE!

Use your CSI journal to keep track of which items glowed under the black light. If you try the light bulbs listed in "Even More to Explore," be sure to keep notes on them as well.

1. Insert the black light lightbulb into the lamp.

2. Place a small amount of each item you will view in its own cup. Label the cups if the materials look similar.

3. Turn off the light. Shine the black light on the materials.

4. Describe how each sample looks in your CSI journal. Which ones glow?

THINK CSI

Got glow? Some materials are fluorescent, meaning they glow when placed under black light. This simple experiment uses a very important and very clever forensic method. Investigators use **ultraviolet** (UV) light to see evidence that can't be seen by eyes alone.

Stains and **latent** fingerprints glow under UV light, for example. UV light technologies are also used to **authenticate** paintings and **signatures**, **analyze** documents, and reveal trace evidence on clothing. And UV light does not destroy the evidence. It just **illuminates** it!

EVEN MORE TO EXPLORE

Expand this experiment using other colored bulbs. Try this activity with some friends. Ask each person to bring a different color of light bulb. Bulbs come in blue, red, yellow, green, and even pink! View the same sample materials using these different-colored lights. What do you see?

CONCLUSION

Take a minute to think about the technology you use in your everyday life.

You know from your own experience that people invent new things almost all the time. This fast-paced march of technology occurs in the field of forensic science as well. Somewhere there's a research lab working hard on a new discovery. Forensic scientists will use this innovation to help solve crimes.

So if you're a budding forensic scientist, keep your eyes and ears open. And be sure to offer **props** to other scientists and engineers! Their hard work continues to expand the forensic science toolkit. And these new tests and technologies might be just what a crime solver needs to catch a thief.

GLOSSARY

analyze – to study the parts of something to discover how it works or what it means.

authenticate – to prove that something is real, not a fake.

botany – the study of plants.

entomology – the study of bugs.

extract – to use a chemical or physical process to obtain part of a substance.

illuminate – to shine a light on something.

latent – being something that is not now visible or active, but may become visible or active.

profile – 1) a summary of data that represents the unique features of someone or something. Also, a graph or similar representation of the data gathered. 2) to create a profile.

props – a slang word meaning respect.

signature – a person's name written in his or her own handwriting.

ultraviolet – a type of light that cannot be seen with the human eye. UV is the abbreviation for *ultraviolet*.

unique – being the only one of its kind.

whodunit – a slang word meaning detective story or mystery story.

INDEX